IN AND ABOUT SALT LAKE CITY

The Mormon Paradise

W. A. MORTON
Publisher
Salt Lake City

British Library Cataloguing-in-Publication Data
A catalogue record for this book is available from the
British Library

THE MORMON TABERNACLE, SALT LAKE CITY

The Tabernacle is an oval-shaped building with an arched roof, resembling the back of a tortoise. It is 250 feet long, 150 feet wide and 80 feet high. About 8,000 people can be comfortably seated within its walls. It is remarkable for its acoustic properties: a low whisper or the dropping of a pin in one end of the building can be heard clearly at the opposite end, 240 feet distant.

ASSEMBLY HALL   TABERNACLE   TEMPLE

THE TEMPLE BLOCK

MORMON ASSEMBLY HALL

Religious meetings not so numerously attended as those of the Tabernacle are usually held in this building. The Assembly Hall is 120 feet long by 68 feet wide, and 130 feet to the top of the central tower. The cost of erection was $90,000.

A SUBURBAN DRIVE

THE LION HOUSE—RESIDENCE OF BRIGHAM YOUNG, BUILT IN 1855.

This is the House in which Brigham Young died, August 29, 1877.

THE PIONEER MONUMENT,

BRIGHAM YOUNG'S GRAVE.

THE ANGEL MORONI

AMELIA PALACE

This House was erected by Brigham Young. who intended to use it as a place of reception for his friends. He died soon after its completion. It is now used as a private residence.

EAGLE GATE

The Eagle Gate was erected by Brigham Young. It was the entrance to his private grounds and also to City Creek Canyon.

SCENE IN COTTONWOOD CANYON

SALT LAKE CITY AND COUNTY BUILDING.

Salt Lake City feels justly proud of its City and County Building, built by the city and county combined at a cost of nearly $300,000. It is 272 feet by 156 feet, the central tower being 250 feet. The structure is built of stone and brick and is fireproof throughout. The grounds are beautifully parked and at night are lighted by electricity.

THE SALT PALACE so named through being covered with crystalized salt, was built as a place of amusement as well as an attraction to visitors, to exhibit Utah's mineral and industrial products. It is situated in the southern part of the city, and may be reached either by State or Main Street car lines.

DR. W. H. GROVES LATTER-DAY SAINTS HOSPITAL

BIRDSEYE VIEW OF SALT LAKE CITY

SALTAIR BEACH PAVILION.

BATHING AT SALTAIR.

THE WASATCH MOUNTAINS, FROM LIBERTY PARK

LAGOON SUMMER RESORT

The Lagoon pleasure resort is situated about twenty miles north of the city. It is reached by the Salt Lake and Ogden Railway.

LEHI SUGAR FACTORY, LEHI, UTAH   MAIN PLANT OF THE UTAH SUGAR COMPANY

This is one of the largest beet sugar factories in America.   The cost of erection was five hundred thousand dollars.   Its output of sugar for 1905 was sixteen million pounds.

BEAR RIVER CANYON.

The famous Bear River canal runs through this canyon and irrigates many thousand acres of land. Bear River is shown in the center of the picture and the Oregon Short Line R. R. on the right.

MERCUR, ONE OF UTAH'S PROSPEROUS MINING CAMPS

EUREKA, UTAH'S FAMOUS MINING CAMP

TOURISTS ON THEIR WAY TO ZION, VIA D & R. G. R. R.

THE OGDEN-LUCIN CUT-OFF—SOUTHERN PACIFIC R. R.

The Cut-off is 100 miles in length, 74 miles on land and 30 miles on trestlework and fill-ins over the waters of Great Salt Lake. The cost was about seven million dollars.

SOME OF THE GREAT SALT BEDS

The waters of the Great Salt Lake carry about twenty per cent. of salt. Around the lake are salt farms, where ponds are formed by building levees, to obtain salt by solar evaporation. This salt is stacked in piles and is ready for market as coarse salt for stock and for the amalgamating works throughout the mining regions.

LOADING THE SALT INTO CARS

About one hundred thousand tons per annum are usually gathered in this way. The salt business in Utah amounts to two hundred thousand dollars per annum.

ECHO CLIFFS.

THE ROYAL GORGE—D. & R. G. RAILWAY.

SEGO LILY UTAH'S STATE FLOWER.

JACKSON SCHOOL, ONE OF SALT LAKE CITY'S PUBLIC SCHOOLS.

SCENES IN OGDEN, UTAH

A UTAH ROUGH RIDER

OLD FOLKS' DAY AT LAGOON, UTAH.

JOSEPH SMITH, THE PROPHET
Born, Dec. 23, 1805.   Assassinated June 27, 1844.

JOSEPH F. SMITH
President of the Church of Jesus Christ of Latter-day Saints.

THE ARTICLES OF FAITH

OF THE CHURCH OF JESUS CHRIST OF LATTER-DAY SAINTS.

1. We believe in God, the Eternal Father, and in His Son Jesus Christ, and in the Holy Ghost.

2. We believe that men will be punished for their own sins and not for Adam's transgression.

3. We believe that through the atonement of Christ, all mankind may be saved, by obedience to the laws and ordinances of the Gospel.

4. We believe that the first principles and ordinances of the Gospel are:—(1) Faith in the Lord Jesus Christ; (2) Repentance; (3) Baptism by immersion for the remission of sins; (4) Laying on of hands for the Gift of the Holy Ghost.

5. We believed that a man must be called of God, by prophecy, and by the laying on of hands, by those who are in authority, to preach the Gospel and administer in the ordinances thereof.

6. We believe in the same organization that existed in the Primitive Church, viz: apostles, prophets, pastors, teachers, evangelists, etc.

7. We believe in the gift of tongues, prophecy, revelation, visions, healing, interpretation of tongues, etc.

8. We believe the Bible to be the word of God, as far as it is translated correctly; we also believe the Book of Mormon to be the word of God.

9. We believe all that God has revealed, all that he does now reveal, and we believe that he will yet reveal many great and important things pertaining to the Kingdom of God.

10. We believe in the literal gathering of Israel, and in the restoration of the Ten Tribes; that Zion will be built upon this (the American) continent: that Christ will reign personally upon the earth; and that the earth will be renewed and receive its paradisaical glory.

11. We claim the privilege of worshiping Almighty God according to the dictates of our concience, and allow all men the same privilage, let them worship how, where, or what they may.

12. We believe in being subject to kings, presidents, rulers, and magistrates, in obeying, honoring, and sustaining the law.

13. We believe in being honest, true, chaste, benevolent, virtuous, and in doing good to *all men*: indeed, we may say that we follow the admonition of Paul, we believe all things, we hope all things, we have endured many things, and hope to be able to endure all things. If there is anything virtuous, lovely, or of good report or praiseworthy, we seek after these things.—JOSEPH SMITH.

A TYPICAL MORMON HYMN.

O MY FATHER.

O my Father, Thou that dwellest
  In the high and glorious place!
When shall I regain Thy presence,
  And again behold Thy face?
In Thy holy habitation,
  Did my spirit once reside!
In my first, primeval childhood,
  Was I nurtured near Thy side!

For a wise and glorious purpose
  Thou hast placed me here on earth,
And withheld the recollection
  Of my former friends and birth.
Yet oft-times a secret something
  Whispered, Your a stranger here,
And I felt that I had wandered
  From a more exalted sphere.

I had learned to call Thee Father,
  Through Thy Spirit from on high
But, until the Key of Knowledge
  Was restored, I knew not why.
In the heavens are parents single?
  No; the thought makes reason stare!
Truth is reason; truth eternal
  Tells me I've a mother there.

When I leave this frail existence,
  When I lay this mortal by,
Father, mother, may I meet you
  In your royal courts on high?
Then at length, when I've completed
  All you sent me forth to do,
With your mutual approbation
  Let me come and dwell with you.

Eliza R. Snow.

| A SKETCH OF | # UTAH AND MORMONISM | BY O. F. WHITNEY |

UTAH owes her existence to a religious movement similar in some of its phases to that which peopled the shores of New England with representatives of the Anglo-Saxon race and laid the foundation of the mightiest government of modern times. No complete history of the United States could be written without some reference to the Pilgrims or Puritans who fled from the persecution in the Old World to find religious freedom in the New. No sketch of Utah would be complete, or even possible, without some reference to the Mormons, or, to give them their proper title, the Church of Jesus Christ of Latter-day Saints; for it was that Church, persecuted in the East and pausing midway in its westward flight from Nauvoo—its last foothold within the confines of civilization—that sent forth the Pioneers who founded Utah, and has ever since furnished the bulk of the bone and sinew that has built up the State. Mormonism and Utah are inseparable themes; as much so as any coupling of cause and effect.

The founder of the Church was Joseph Smith, a native of Vermont, who as a boy of fourteen, in the forest fringed districts of Western New York, received visitations from on high, apprising him of the apostate condition of Christendom and authorizing him to establish anew upon earth the true Church of Christ. His first visitation was in the spring of 1820, when the Father and Son appeared to him, opening the new gospel dispensation. Subsequently he was visited by an angel named Moroni, who revealed to him the existence of some golden plates, hidden in a hill near the village of Manchester. These plates, temporarily entrusted to him by the angel, were covered with ancient hieroglyphics, which Joseph Smith, by means of the Urim and Thummim—also delivered to him by the angel—translated, and gave to the world as a result the Book of Mormon. It is a record of the ancient inhabitants of America, from the time of the Tower of Babel down to the early part of the fifth century of the Christian Era, and is mostly the history of a people called Nephites, a branch of the house of Israel, who, led by Lehi and his son Nephi, of the tribe of Manassah, and followed by some of the children of Judah, came from Jerusalem about the year 600 B. C. and peopled South and North America. To these descendants of Abraham the Savior appeared, after his resurrection, and taught the fulness of his Gospel, supplementing and preceding the teachings of other prophets, the last of whom was Moroni, afterwards the angel custodian of the golden plates, who, while yet a mortal, about 420 A. D., hid them in the hill from which they were taken by Joseph Smith. This place of deposit was called by the Nephites, Cumorah. The Book of Mormon takes its name from Mormon, the father of Moroni, who recorded upon the plates the history of his people, the white progenitors of the dusky and degenerate American Indians.

Among the angelic visitants connected with the rise of the Latter-day Church, was John the Baptist, who, on May 15, 1829, conferred upon Joseph Smith and Oliver Cowdery the Aaronic Priesthood, empowering them to preach faith and repentance and to baptize by immersion for the remission of sins. This was followed by a visitation from Peter, James and John, who conferred upon Joseph and Oliver the Melchisedek Priesthood, which gave them power to bestow the Holy Ghost by the laying on of hands.

Thus equipped with the Bible and Book of Mormon as their doctrinal standards, supplemented by immediate and continuous revelation, this twain—known as the First and Second Elders of the Church—with others ordained by them, went forth preaching amid the hottest persecution the restored gospel, healing the sick, casting out devils, and otherwise "confirming the words with signs following." Their first converts were made from Western and Southern New York and Northern Pennsylvania.

The Church of Jesus Christ of Latter-day Saints—nicknamed "Mormons" for their belief in the Book of Mormon—was organized at Fayette, Seneca County, New York, on the 6th day of April, 1830. Within a year it moved bodily to Kirtland, Ohio, which became during the next seven years its headquarters. In 1831, it established a colony in Jackson County, Missouri, the site of the future City of Zion, the New Jerusalem, which the Saints, who are of Israel, mostly of the seed of Ephraim, gathered out from all nations, expect to rear in fulfillment of prophecy, preparatory to the second coming of the Savior.

Persecution followed them both to Ohio and Missouri. In the fall of 1833 they were expelled with fire and sword from Jackson County, and early in 1838 the main body of the Church, having lost some of its prominent members by apostasy, abandoned Kirtland, with the temple they had built there, and concentrated twelve to fifteen thousand strong, in and around Caldwell County, Missouri, where they founded Far West and other flourishing settlements. There trouble again arose, caused by religious and political differences between them and the other settlers, and in the fall and winter succeeding, the Jackson County tragedy was repeated on a larger scale. Under on order issued by Governor Lilburn W. Boggs, and executed by Major-General John B. Clark and others, in command of an overwhelming force of militia, the entire Mormon community, after many of them had been killed in battle and massacred, their leaders imprisoned, their homes devastated, were driven in mid-winter from the confines of the State.

Kindly received by the people of Illinois, the expatriated community settled on the east shore of the Mississippi, in Hancock County, where they founded their beautiful city of Nauvoo, surrounded by other Mormon settlements, both in Illinois and Iowa. There they remained for seven years, increasing rapidly by immigration from the Eastern States, Canada and Great Britain until they aggregated twenty thousand souls. Religious and political animosity still pursued them, and finally on the 27th day of June, 1844, their Prophet Joseph Smith, and his brother Hyrum, the Patriarch of the Church, who had surrendered for trial on a trumped up charge of treason and riot, were murdered in Carthage jail by an anti-Mormon mob, while under the pledged protection of the Governor of the State. Justice was never done on the murderers.

Under Brigham Young, the successor to Joseph Smith, the Mormon people, in February, 1846, began the famous exodus from Illinois, leaving Nauvoo with its Temple, which had just been dedicated, to be pillaged and desecrated by their enemies. From their scattered camps in Iowa, and on the Missouri, in the summer of that year, went forth at the call of their country the Mormon Battalion, 500 strong, to assist the United States in its war against Mexico. In the spring of 1847 the Mormon pioneers (one hundred and forty three men, three women and two children) led by Brigham Young in person, leaving the main body encamped upon the frontier, started upon their historic journey to the Rocky Mountains. Traversing trackless plains and snow-clad mountains lying between the Missouri river and the great American Desert, on the 24th day of July they entered Salt Lake Valley, where, in the midst of desolation, surrounded by savage tribes and suffering untold hardships and privation, they founded Salt Lake City, the metropolis of the Inter-Mountain region; the parent of more than two hundred cities, towns and villages, that owe their existence to the Mormon people and their great leader, Brigham Young. The residue of the migrating Church followed the Pioneers to their new-found home in the wilderness; thenceforth the gathering place of the Mormon people.